I0146157

THIS WE PRAY

SEA OF PEOPLE

This We Pray | Sea of People

W. Nikola-Lisa

Gyroscope Books

Chicago

Copyright 2020 W. Nikola-Lisa
Published by Gyroscope Books, Chicago
For information about permission to reproduce
selections from this book, please email the author
at nikolabooks@gmail.com

For orders by U.S. trade bookstores, retail outlets, and public libraries,
please contact the Ingram Content Group: Retail (800) 937-8000,
Libraries (800) 937-5300, or visit www.ingramcontent.com

Photo Credits: All photo montages created from non-editorial content licensed from shutterstock.com.
Artists work used for *This We Pray* include: Ahturner, Aldo Risolvo, ArtMari, Cheryl Casey, Djomas, Ebtikar, Everything Is Stock, fizkes, FotoMikv, Helen Sushitskaya, Horn Andrey, IVY PHOTOS, Kamira, Laurin Rinder, Lotus_studio, Monkey Business Images, panitanphoto, Prostock-studio, Rawpixel, Rikesh Attadip, Roxana Gonzalez, se media, shutterupeire, spixel, StockPhotosArt, Thomas Dutour, Victor Naumik, and WAYHOME studio. Artists work used for *Sea of People* include: AlessandroBiascioli, Alexey Skachkov, DisobeyArt, Drazen Zigic, Halfpoint, Jacob Lund, Ju1978, Pino Mastrullo, Rawpixel, Red Marker, Ufuk Aydin, and VAKS-Stock Agency. Front Cover Art: Horn Andrey and ArtMari. Back Cover Art: DisobeyArt.

Publisher's Cataloging-In-Publication Data
(Prepared by The Donahue Group, Inc.)

Names: Nikola-Lisa, W., author.
Title: This we pray ; Sea of people / W. Nikola-Lisa.
Other Titles: Sea of people.
Description: Chicago : Gyroscope Books, [2020]
Identifiers: ISBN 9781734192339 (hardcover) | ISBN 9781734192346 (paperback) |
    ISBN 9781734192353 (ebook)
Subjects: LCSH: Prayer--Poetry. | Social action--Poetry. | LCGFT: Poetry.
Classification: LCC PS3564.I373 T45 2020 (print) | LCC PS3564.I373 (ebook) | DDC 811/.54—dc23

*Dedicated to those whose lives
have been lost to senseless violence*

*And to their loved ones whose lives
have been changed by it forever*

Foreword

The times demand a response. Some people prefer prayer and contemplation. Others prefer action. Both are acts of civil disobedience in their own right, just at opposite ends of the spectrum. Over the years however, I've come to believe that both are indispensable, that they are two sides of the same coin, distinct but inseparable. Prayer can be a powerful tool, but slow in its effect. I'm reminded of the saying, often expressed by Dr. Martin Luther King, Jr., "The arc of the moral universe is long, but it bends toward justice." It does, but very slowly. Hence, the call to action. But action without contemplation is easily led off course, frequently into wanton destruction and violence. To constrain that tendency, prayer and contemplation are essential, for they provide the moral ground for "right action," action that is positive, peaceful, and progressive. It is with this in mind that I offer these seemingly disparate reflections of the challenging times in which we live.

THIS WE PRAY

It's a sad, sad thing—

a brother is killed.

A sister weeps.

A mother wails.

A father clenches his fists

and walks away.

A cousin sobs.

An aunt moans.

An uncle calls out,

"Oh, no."

A neighbor sighs.

A friend cries.

Others shake their heads

   in disbelief.

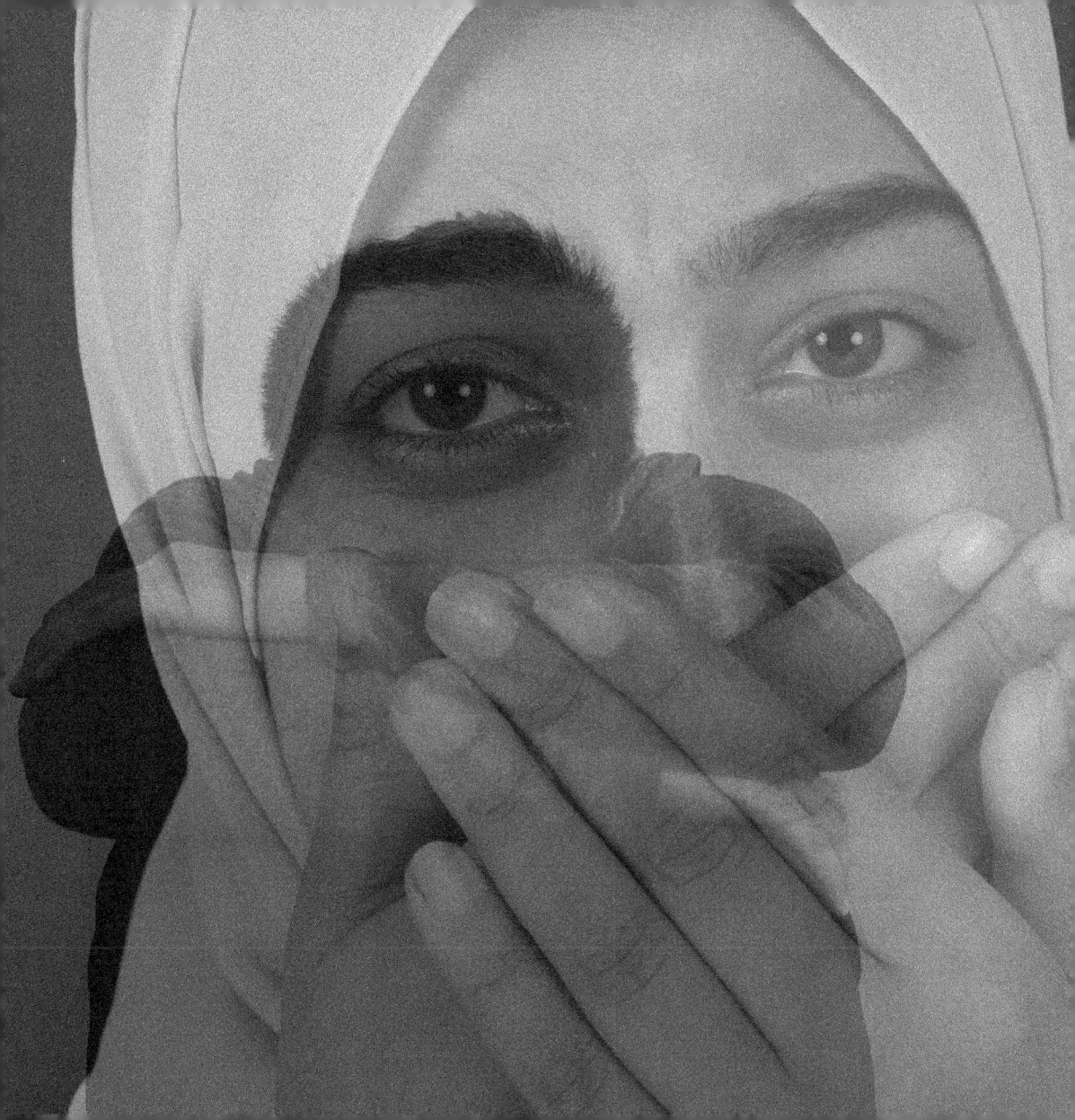

One by one,

    they take their leave.

One by one,

    they say good-bye.

One by one,

    they ask themselves...

Why?

Why has this come to pass?

What?

What sense does it all make?

How?

How long shall the killing be?

Yes, a brother is killed,

laid down to rest

long before his time,

and it's a sad, sad thing—

a life gone just like that.

Pray, oh Lord,

pray it'll stop soon.

Pray, oh Lord,

pray it'll go away.

Pray, oh Lord,

that out of this hardship,

these bitter tears,

we learn...

to be together,

to live together,

to care for one another,

and to love.

Yes, this we pray, oh Lord.

This we pray.

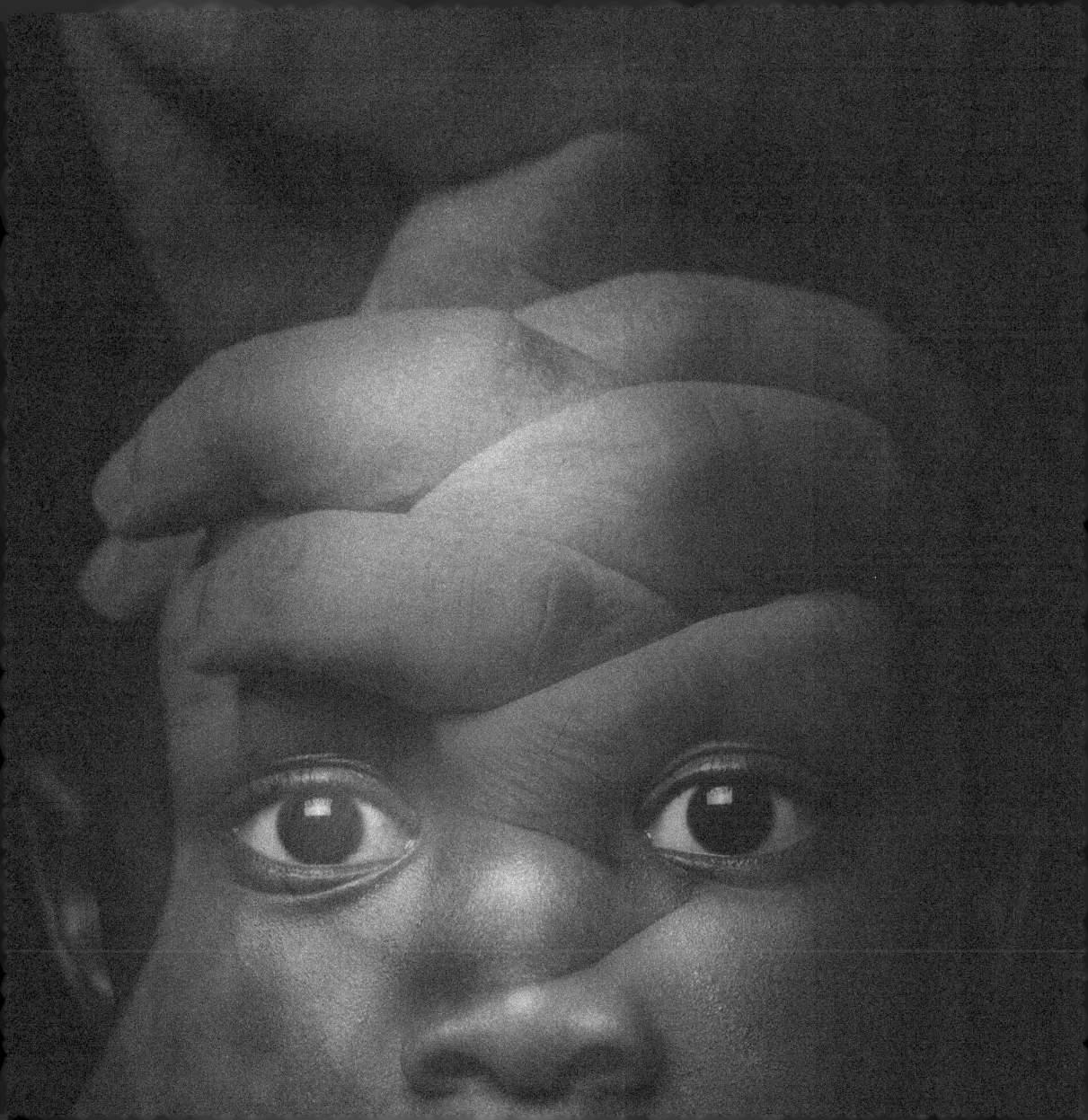

Amen.

SEA OF PEOPLE

sea of people
break of dawn
gathered on
the nation's lawn

sea of people
Sunday best
come to put
the past to rest

sea of people
common cause
here to heal
the nation's laws

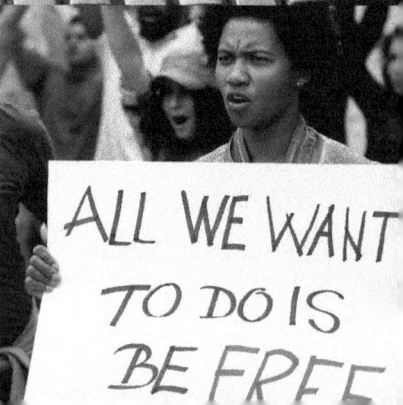

ALL WE WANT
TO DO IS
BE FREE

sea of people
forming lines
Freedom Now
demand their signs

sea of people
young and old
standing tall
acting bold

sea of people
moral force
out to change
the nation's course

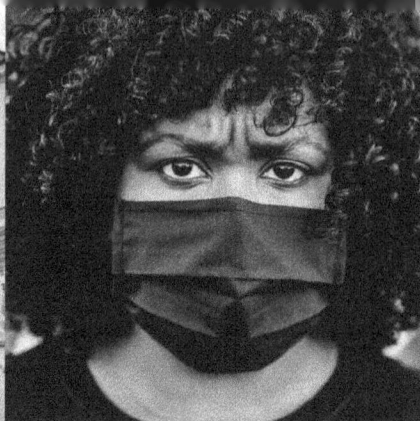

sea of people
human braid
show the world
they're not afraid

sea of people
black and white
linking arms
to lead the fight

sea of people
hearts on fire
filled with hope
that will not tire

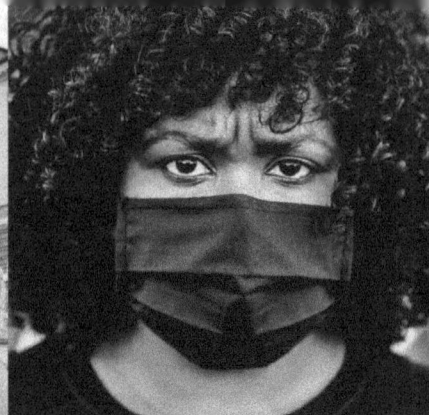

sea of people
mighty stream
come to hear
their leader's dream

sea of people
moved to tears
moved by words
beyond their fears

sea of people
wall of will
faith renewed
on freedom's hill

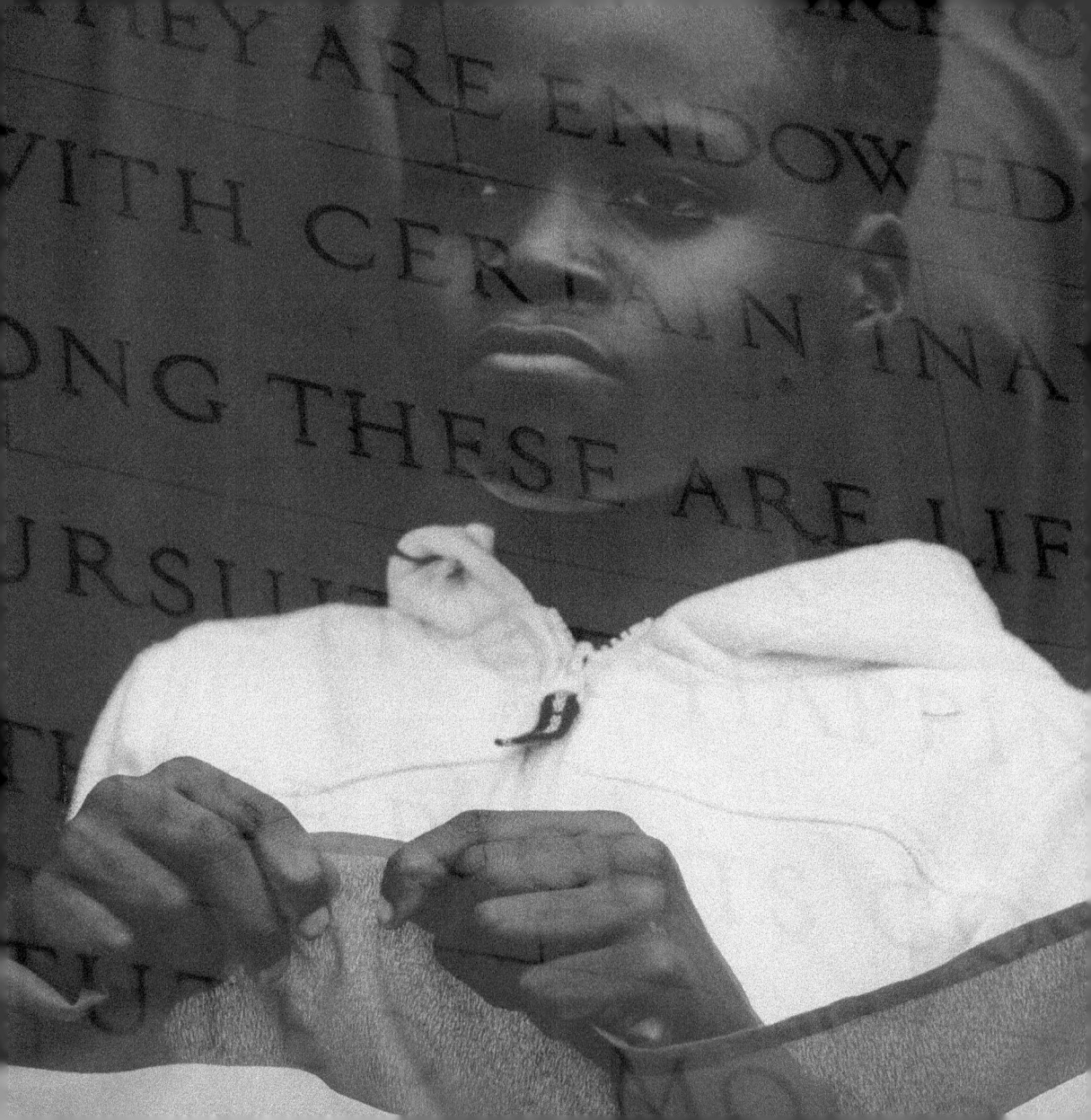

Afterword

In our collective attempt to form "a more perfect Union," one day, hopefully, we will be able to say that all lives matter. Unfortunately, that day has not arrived, and it will not arrive until we are able to say—openly, honestly, sincerely—that Black lives matter (and Brown lives, and Red lives; in other words, the lives of all people of color). Until that day, we have work to do, both as individuals and as a society. So let's get to it, let's get the work done, so that our children's children can look back with pride and admiration, as we do to our forefathers and mothers, and say that we were the greatest generation ever.

W. Nikola-Lisa is the author of over thirty books for readers young and old. His books include *Bein' With You This Way*, *How We Are Smart*, *The Men Who Made the Yankees*, and the award-winning *Dog Eared: A Year's Romp Through the Self-Publishing World*. Find out more about the author and his work at www.nikolabooks.com.

Also by the author, *Please Don't Say An X Word*, a unique springboard for parents, teachers, and caregivers to talk to children about swearing. Winner of an Independent Press Award for an "all ages" picture book.

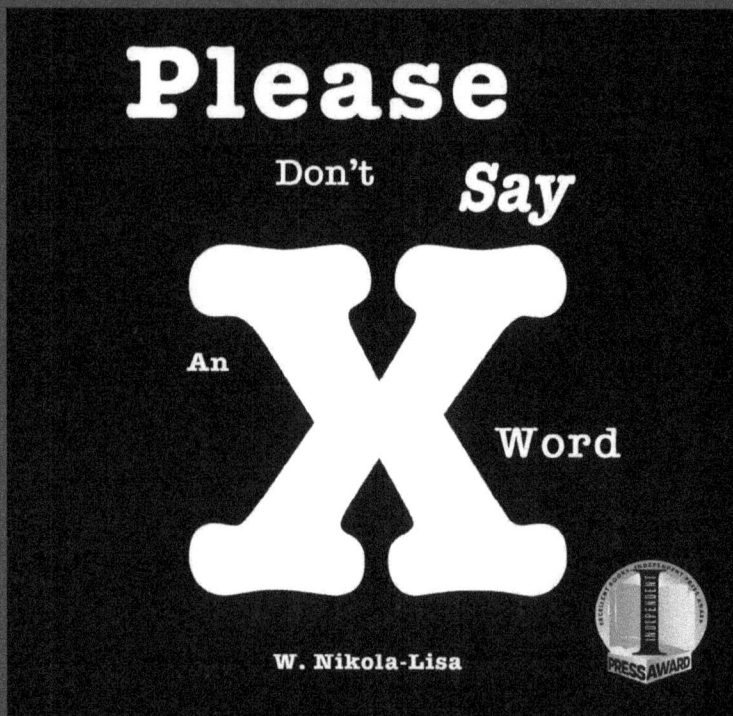

Please
Don't   ## Say
An
X
Word

W. Nikola-Lisa

This book will be a wonderful teaching method to teach kids not to use words to bully. Meena Naik

A great choice for parents of conscientious children. Sephi Coleman Tunney

www.ingramcontent.com/pod-product-compliance
Lightning Source LLC
Chambersburg PA
CBHW042350030426
42336CB00025B/3436